CORE SKILLS

# PRESENT IT:
## UNDERSTANDING CONTEXTS AND AUDIENCES

**Miriam Coleman**

**PowerKiDS** press™

New York

Published in 2013 by The Rosen Publishing Group, Inc.
29 East 21st Street, New York, NY 10010

First Edition

Editor: Joanne Randolph
Book Design: Kate Laczynski
Layout Design: Holly Rankin

Photo Credits: Cover, p. 6 Brand X Pictures/Thinkstock; p. 4 Dirk Anschutz/Stone/Getty Images; p. 5 AVAVA/Shutterstock.com; p. 7 Mary Kate Denny/Stone/Getty Images; p. 8 Image Source/Thinkstock; p. 9 Rob Daugherty/Flickr/Getty Images; p. 10 Kean Collection/Archive Photos/Getty Images; p. 11 Dorling Kindersley RF/Thinkstock; p. 12 Peter Dazeley/Photographer's Choice/Getty Images; pp. 13, 17 iStockphoto/Thinkstock; p. 15 Morgan Lane Photography/Shutterstock.com; p. 16 © iStockphoto.com/ Deborah Cheramie; p. 18 Jupiterimages/FoodPix/Getty Images; p. 19 Kamira/Shutterstock.com; p. 20 Carey Kirkella/Taxi/Getty Images; p. 21 Stephen Simpson/The Image Bank/Getty Images; p. 22 Cultura/ Hybrid Images/StockImages/Getty Images; p. 23 Siri Stafford/Taxi/Getty Images; p. 24 Steve Gorton/ Dorling Kindersley/Getty Images; p. 25 Camille Tokeud Photography Inc./Workbook Stock/Getty Images; p. 26 Stephen Simpson/Iconica/Getty Images; p. 27 © iStockphoto.com/Jasmina; p. 28 Tim Platt/ Iconica/Getty Images; p. 29 Olga Lyubkina/Shutterstock.com; p. 30 Jamie Grill/Iconica/Getty Images.

Library of Congress Cataloging-in-Publication Data

Coleman, Miriam.
 Present it : understanding contexts and audiences / by Miriam Coleman. — 1st ed.
     p. cm. —  (Core skills)
 Includes index.
 ISBN 978-1-4488-7455-2 (library binding) — ISBN 978-1-4488-7527-6 (pbk.) —
 ISBN 978-1-4488-7602-0 (6-pack)
 1.  Public speaking—Juvenile literature. 2.  Report writing—Juvenile literature. I. Title.
 PN4129.15.C62 2013
 808.5'1—dc23

2012008061

Manufactured in the United States of America

CPSIA Compliance Information: Batch #SW12PK: For Further Information contact Rosen Publishing, New York, New York at 1-800-237-9932

# Contents

# WHAT IS A PRESENTATION?

When you share what you have learned with others, you are making a presentation. A presentation is a great way to show what you have learned and put new ideas together. A presentation can take many forms, from a simple written report to a movie that you write and produce.

*Have you ever sat in the auditorium of your school to watch a play or listen to a talk about how to stop bullying? The school auditorium is a place where people give presentations to big groups.*

Whatever kind of presentation you make, it is always important to think about how to make the information both clear and interesting. If someone were presenting this information to you, what would catch your attention? What would make you want to learn more about the subject? What would confuse you or just put you to sleep?

# WHO IS YOUR AUDIENCE?

When you make a presentation, you should always think about who the **audience** will be for the final product. Will you present to just your teacher or your whole class? Will the presentation be to a panel of judges at a science fair?

*At a science fair, you are presenting to teachers, parents, and other students. You will need a display to show what your topic is and what you have learned. You will also need to know enough about your topic to speak comfortably about it to many people.*

Think about how much your audience already knows about the subject on which you are presenting. If you are making a presentation to people who know nothing about the subject, you may need to **define** and carefully explain things that might seem basic to you. If you are making a presentation to people who are already experts on the subject, you might not need to explain those basics. You will, however, want to show what a **unique** understanding you have gained about the topic.

Think about what kind of language will best explain the information to your audience. Will scientific terms need to be explained? If you use words from another language, will you need to translate them?

# WHAT ARE YOU TRYING TO SAY?

Before you begin writing or drawing up your presentation, think about what you want your work to say. First of all, what are the requirements of your assignment? If this is a **research** project, what are your research goals?

Let's say you want to present information on the fact that the black rhinoceros is endangered. You could present this information using words, or you might decide to use a bar graph to show how much this animal's numbers have dropped over time.

Ask yourself basic questions, such as who, what, when, where, why, and how? What is the most important information that you want your audience to learn? What are your main ideas? Think about what the facts or statements you make mean to you and how they fit together.

*Your teacher might ask you to compare the real story of Pocahontas with popular stories and movies about her life. Once you decide what you want to say, you can put your data into a chart or Venn diagram.*

# THE NITROGEN CYCLE

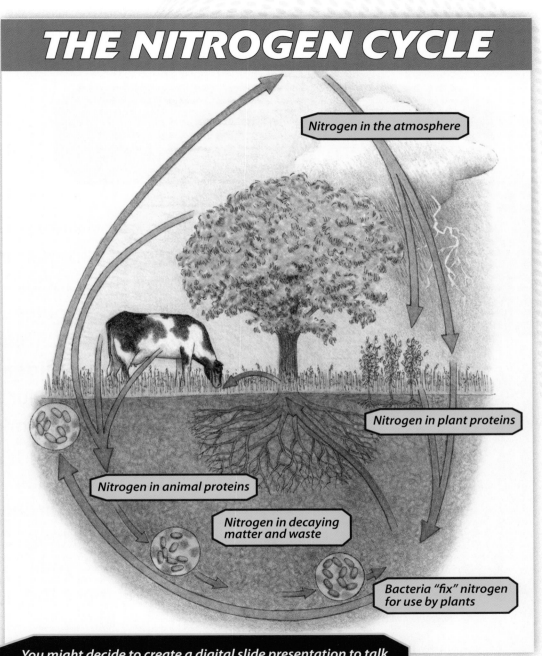

Nitrogen in the atmosphere

Nitrogen in plant proteins

Nitrogen in animal proteins

Nitrogen in decaying matter and waste

Bacteria "fix" nitrogen for use by plants

You might decide to create a digital slide presentation to talk about the nitrogen cycle. You could include slides with facts and a slide with a diagram to show how this cycle works.

Use many different sources of information on your topic, including books, digital sources, and other media. Think about how the **evidence** you see supports your main ideas. As you work on your presentation, clearly state your main ideas and the supporting evidence. This will help bring structure to your work and will make the presentation easier for your audience to follow.

# KINDS OF PRESENTATIONS

There are many different ways of presenting the information you have learned. Each type of presentation requires different skills and **strategies**.

## QUICK TIP

No matter what kind of presentation you are making, it is always important to put things in your own words and give credit to the sources of information you are using.

*For any kind of presentation, you will want to take notes as you plan your project and do research.*

13

*Using a word-processing program to type up a written report will help make your paper easy for your teacher to read. Word-processing programs also have tools that let you easily insert charts, diagrams, and pictures.*

## QUICK TIP
**Have someone else read over what you have written to double-check for any typos and other errors.**

## Written Presentations

When doing a written presentation, you will write out what you have learned and hand it in for your teacher to read. It is very important to write clearly and **precisely** and to be careful to use correct spelling and grammar.

You will need to create a structure for your written presentation that introduces the topic clearly and then develops it with details and evidence that are grouped together in a logical order. You may want to use special formatting features, such as headings, to separate different parts of your report. You will also need to **cite** your sources in a proper format, whether you are using parenthetical citations, endnotes, footnotes, or a bibliography.

*In science, ideas and theories must be proved using methods that others can repeat to get the same results. Demonstrating what you have learned about something helps prove that your idea is correct.*

## Oral Presentations

When doing oral presentations, you must stand up and talk about what you have learned. Speaking clearly and confidently is important in an oral presentation. You need to create an orderly structure so that your listeners can follow your line of thought, just as you do for written presentations. You may

Let's say you are learning about the Mohs' scale of hardness in a unit on rocks. The teacher may ask you to demonstrate how it works for the class.

*Giving an oral presentation might make you nervous, but if you have prepared and done good research, you should feel good about it. Remember, too, that everyone else in the class likely feels nervous!*

also need to be prepared to respond to what your audience has to say.

## Demonstrations

Demonstrations are a kind of oral presentation during which you perform an experiment in front of a group to demonstrate a scientific principle or theory. Like all presentations, demonstrations require a great deal of preparation before the big event. You will need to research the science you are demonstrating so that you can properly explain the reasons behind the effects your demonstration will produce.

# MAKING WRITTEN REPORTS STAND OUT

The first step in making a written report stand out is in the way you use language. Grab your readers' attention with vivid descriptions or by introducing your topic in a creative way. Use vocabulary that is specific to your topic. Include quotes from authorities on the subject.

For a written report on Mexico, you could make tamales or another typical food with your family. Take a photo of the meal you make and insert it into your project.

Adding drawings, charts, maps, and diagrams to a written report can help it stand out, too. These kind of tools present information visually, which can add depth to a report.

If you are writing about a historical topic or another culture, quote from primary sources such as diaries, letters, or news accounts from the time or place. Some projects could be made livelier by including **dialogue**. Always make sure to be as precise and clear as possible.

Drawing relevant examples from your own experience can really make a written report stand out.

*Have a parent read through your report to make sure you have not made any mistakes. Your parent can let you know if any of your ideas are unclear, too.*

Finding comparisons and examples from current events that you read about in a newspaper or magazine or even from novels or poetry can do so as well. Making connections to these experiences or other texts shows that you understand your topic and are able to integrate it with what you learn from other sources.

If you are doing a project on ocean habitats, you could visit an aquarium to learn more about your topic. Hands-on experiences will help you feel more engaged with your topic, which should shine through in your final report.

You can also use illustrations such as photographs, drawings, and charts to help share your information in a written presentation. You could even include recipes or step-by-step instructions for completing a task. Think creatively about what kinds of information will help present a full portrait of your subject.

# MAKING ORAL REPORTS STAND OUT

Holding the attention of your audience is one of your most important tasks when you give an oral presentation. Simply standing up and **summarizing** facts can make it hard for the audience to absorb the information. How can you make your oral report stand out?

Sometimes you might be asked to give a group oral report. You will want to divide the work within your group and then leave time to come together to practice presenting what you have found together.

If you are giving an oral report about the early explorers, you could make a model ship to highlight what you have learned.

Just as in a written report, using illustrations in an oral report can help tell your story. You can draw these yourself on large pieces of poster board or use a projector, television screen, or computer to display photographs or charts.

When doing oral presentations, you can also use other media like audio and video clips to engage

You could give your classmates a fun quiz at the end of your report. If a lot of people know the answers, you will know you did a good job presenting the data on your topic!

your audience. An oral presentation about the civil rights movement could **incorporate** protest songs from that era, recordings of interviews with people who were there, or old news footage from that time.

Encouraging your audience to participate is another great way to get them to pay attention. Try holding a question and answer session when you have finished giving your report. You can also pass around objects to involve the audience. If you are writing about another culture, share food that the audience can taste or pass around musical instruments to play with.

*If you are doing an oral report on someone in your family, you can make a video or an audio recording of your interview. You could also share old photos of your family member with the class.*

# USING DIGITAL TOOLS IN YOUR PRESENTATION

Digital tools can be useful in every stage of your presentation. Digital research tools like search engines, electronic card catalogs, e-books, and online databases can help you find a variety of sources from which to draw information for your project.

*Your library likely has access to lots of digital tools, such as e-books and databases, to help you research. Its computers probably have word-processing programs that you can use to type up what you have learned and make a polished finished product, too.*

*Making a video in which you talk about your topic can be a fun way to present information. Remember that you still need to give facts and come up with a well-rounded report backed by evidence.*

Communication tools such as e-mail, file-sharing programs, and video conferencing can help you work with a team on group presentations. They can also help you find and communicate with sources who can provide information.

For the final product, digital tools can help you incorporate **multimedia** displays into your presentations to help make them stand out. There are digital tools that can help you create infographics, such as charts and maps, to illustrate information in both written and oral presentations.

*There are many digital tools that can help you create graphic organizers and infographics, such as pie charts and bar graphs, to share what you have learned on a topic.*

*If you are doing a report on grasshoppers, you can go on a bug hunt with your parent and take a picture of what you find. Most word-processing programs let you upload photos and easily insert them into your paper.*

Digital files of audio and video recordings make it easy to include valuable and interesting information. Programs such as PowerPoint can help you create slideshows to present both text and illustrations to your audience in a fun and engaging style. If you want to share your presentation with a larger audience, you can use web tools to create a website or blog for your project.

# BE CREATIVE!

*Presenting your work to the class should be a learning experience for you as well as your audience. How will you tackle your next presentation?*

Making a presentation gives you a chance to think about what you are learning in a new way. What are the most important things you have learned about your topic? How can you make the topic interesting to other people? Presentations give you a chance to get creative while putting together facts and ideas.

Being creative in your approach to a topic actually helps you learn more. By spending the time to think of a new approach, you are integrating ideas from many sources. When doing this, your brain makes important connections. This is how we learn. When we present what we have learned to others, we are creating a community with shared ideas and knowledge. Presenting is powerful!

# Glossary

**audience** (AH-dee-ints)  A group of people who watch, read, or listen to something.

**cite** (SYT)  To call attention to or give credit to a source.

**define** (dih-FYN)  To give meaning to something.

**dialogue** (DY-uh-log)  A conversation between two or more people.

**evidence** (EH-vuh-dunts)  Facts that prove something.

**incorporate** (in-KOR-puh-rayt) To blend into or combine with something.

**multimedia** (mul-tee-MEE-dee-uh)  Using more than one kind of communication.

**precisely** (prih-SYS-lee)  Exactly.

**research** (REE-serch)  Having to do with study.

**strategies** (STRA-tuh-jeez)  Carefully made plans or methods.

**summarizing** (SUH-muh-ryz-ing)  Making a short account of something that has been said or written.

**unique** (yoo-NEEK)  One of a kind.

# Index

# Websites

Due to the changing nature of Internet links, PowerKids Press has developed an online list of websites related to the subject of this book. This site is updated regularly. Please use this link to access the list:
www.powerkidslinks.com/cs/present/